#birthday

a quote book

by gloria marie pelcher

Copyright © 2014 Gloria Marie Pelcher

All rights reserved. No portion of this book may be used or reproduced in any manner whatsoever without written permission of the author or Creative Bluebird except in the case of brief quotations embodied in critical articles and reviews.

The quotes in this book have been collected from multiple sources, and are assumed to be accurate as quoted in their original published forms. Although every effort has been made to verify the quotes and sources, the Publisher cannot guarantee their perfect accuracy. No endorsement of this book has been made by any individual mentioned in this quote book.

#birthday: a quote book

ISBN-13: 978-0692346808 (Creative Bluebird)

ISBN-10: 0692346805

#quotebooks™ is a trademark of

Creative Bluebird
www.creativebluebird.com

For book inquiries please visit
creativebluebird.com/contact

for

___

from

___

date

___

#birthday

Here's to being you and living your life to the fullest! Happy Birthday!

It takes courage to grow up and become who you really are.

        E.E. Cummings

Be yourself; everyone else is already taken.

Oscar Wilde

With mirth and laughter let old wrinkles come.

William Shakespeare

Deer do not fret over passing birthdays. an alone measures time. Man alone chimes the hour. And, because of this, man alone suffers a paralyzing fear that no other creature endures. A fear of time running out.

Mitch Albom

The year you were born marks only your entry into the world. Other years where you prove your worth, they are the ones worth celebrating.

Jarod Kintz

Wish on everything. Pink cars are good, especially old ones. And stars of course, first stars and shooting stars. Planes will do if they are the first light in the sky and look like stars. Wish in tunnels, holding your breath and lifting your feet off the ground. Birthday candles. Baby teeth.

Francesca Lia Block

A slice of cake never made anyone fat.

Jeanne Ray

The way I see it, you should live everyday like it is your birthday.

                                                   Paris Hilton

You know you're getting old when the candles cost more than the cake.
Bob Hope

Last week the candle factory burned down. Everyone just stood around and sang, "Happy Birthday".

Steven Wright

All I want for my birthday is another birthday.

Ian Dury

If you're blessed enough to grow older, there's so much wisdom to be gained from celebrating the process with vibrancy and vigor and grace.
Oprah Winfrey

Some day you will be old enough to start reading fairy tales again.

C.S. Lewis

…There would have been more I love yous ... more I'm sorrys ... more I'm listenings ... but mostly, given another shot at life, I would seize every minute of it ... look at it and really see it ... try it on ... live it ... exhaust it ... and never give that minute back until there was nothing left of it.

Erma Bombeck

You've gotta dance like there's nobody watching,
Love like you'll never be hurt,
Sing like there's nobody listening,
And live like it's heaven on earth.
William W. Purkey

When you chase a dream, you learn about yourself. You learn your capabilities and limitations, and the value of hard work and persistence.

Nicholas Sparks

To live is the rarest thing in the world. Most people exist, that is all.

Oscar Wilde

If Joan of Arc could turn the tide of an entire war before her eighteenth birthday, you can get out of bed.

                                              E. Jean Carroll

Youth is the gift of nature,
but age is the work of art.
 Garson Kanin

Wrinkles should merely indicate where smiles have been.

Mark Twain

Youthfulness is about how you live not when you were born.

Karl Lagerfeld

Count your age by friends, not years. Count your life by smiles, not tears.

         John Lennon

Be brave enough to live creatively. The creative is the place where no one else has ever been. You have to leave the city of your comfort and go into the wilderness of your intuition. You cannot get there by bus, only by hard work, risking and by not quite knowing what you are doing. What you will discover will be wonderful: Yourself.

Alan Alda

I am not young enough to know everything.

Oscar Wilde

Laughter is timeless.
Imagination has no age. And
dreams are forever.

Walt Disney Company

Another belief of mine: that everyone else my age is an adult, whereas I am merely in disguise.
Margaret Atwood

Aging is not 'lost youth' but a new stage of opportunity and strength.

Betty Friedan

We'll never be as young as we are tonight.

Chuck Palahniuk

Most people don't grow up. Most people age. They find parking spaces, honor their credit cards, get married, have children, and call that maturity. What that is, is aging.
Maya Angelou

If you live to be one hundred, you've got it made. Very few people die past that age.

George Burns

Spring passes and one remembers one's innocence.
Summer passes and one remembers one's exuberance.
Autumn passes and one remembers one's reverence.
Winter passes and one remembers one's perseverance.
Yoko Ono

...inside every old person is a young person wondering what happened.

Terry Pratchett

If my life is going to mean anything,
I have to live it myself.

Rick Riordan

The secret of genius is to carry the spirit of the child into old age, which means never losing your enthusiasm.

Aldous Huxley

So what if nobody came?
I'll have all the ice cream and tea,
And I'll laugh with myself,
And I'll dance with myself,
And I'll sing, "Happy Birthday to me!"
Shel Silverstein

The cake had a trick candle that wouldn't go out, so I didn't get my wish. Which was just that it would always be like this, that my life could be a party just for me.

Janet Fitch

A happy birthday is measured not in the amount of gifts one gets, but in the amount one is loved.

Todd Stocker

birthday

There are only two ways to live your life. One is as though nothing is a miracle. The other is as though everything is a miracle.

Albert Einstein

I'm the one that's got to die when it's time for me to die, so let me live my life the way I want to.

Jimi Hendrix

May you live every day of your life.

Jonathan Swift

At the age of six I wanted to be a cook. At seven I wanted to be Napoleon. And my ambition has been growing steadily ever since.

Salvador Dalí

Age isn't how old you are but how old you feel.

Gabriel Garcí-a Márquez

When people talk about the good old days, I say to people, 'It's not the days that are old, it's you that's old.' I hate the good old days. What is important is that today is good.

Karl Lagerfeld

Every year on your birthday,
you get a chance to start new.
Sammy Hagar

I'm gonna enjoy being old
I think I'll be awesome at
it.

                                            Craig Ferguson

Those who succeed in an outstanding way seldom do so before the age of 40. More often, they do not strike their real pace until they are well beyond the age of 50.

Napoleon Hill

It is a mistake to regard age as a downhill grade toward dissolution. The reverse is true. As one grows older, one climbs with surprising strides.

George Sand

With age comes wisdom, but sometimes age comes alone.
Oscar Wilde

The way I see it, you should live everyday like it is your birthday.

Paris Hilton

There are two great days in a person's life – the day we are born and the day we discover why.

William Barclay

my favorite birthday quote

_____
_____
_____
_____
_____
_____
_____
_____
_____
_____

A B O U T this book

THIS BOOK that you are holding in your hands was made with love by GLORIA MARIE PELCHER. This book is part of the *#quotebooks*™ collection of books. This book is perfectly okay with being loved, bought, read, reread, shared, gifted, tweeted, instagrammed, liked, reviewed, borrowed, and of course quoted.

gloriamarie.com/quotebooks

FB / IG / Twitter: @gloriamarie